THE CIRCLE

THE CIRCLE

Tales of Spring Lake Road
Columbia, SC

PALMETTO

PUBLISHING

Charleston, SC
www.PalmettoPublishing.com

Hardcover ISBN: 9798822961371
Paperback ISBN: 9798822961388

Christmas tree image courtesy of Flaticon.com
Duckling image courtesy of wirestock on Freepik

We would like to acknowledge and thank the following Spring Lake Residents for their help in publishing this history. Their memories and stories of times shared on the Circle over the years have been invaluable.

We do thank you!
Linda Gillespie and Sharon Vanzant

Committee Members:
Sally Pulliam, Sandy Shull Roberts, Sassy Shull
and Libby Rush Tompkins

We also give special thanks to Brittney Evans for her document support and helpful research for The Circle, Tales of Spring Lake Road.

Table of Contents

Spring Lake Road, In Spring

Boston has its fine Brookline,
And Frisco its Nob Hill…
Philly has its old Main Line,
So take your choice, at will;
Through them all at length I've ridden,
When I was by my host bidden,
And none there can compare
As the finest for abode
To Columbia's Springlake Road.

Winding by the golf course, green,
Stately…quiet…and serene,
Where the homes fit in that scene-
Lovely, every season through,
Appearing neither old nor new,
Each with spacious, well-kept lawn,
Even if the owner's gone,
The owners all portray their scene,
For they are elegant…serene.
In the spring when flowers bloom,
Here there is no room for gloom,
Those then viewing each abode
Find no place like Springlake Road.

Anonymous
Columbia, SC
Sept. 30, 1982

THE BEGINNING

First Families

Spring Lake Circle became the circle it is today in the late 1940's and early 1950's. The first families to buy lots out here could be called adventurers since this area was considered too far outside the city of Columbia.

One of the first group of families to build on the Circle were Bill and Gretchen Dawson, Rudy and Dee Gayden, Jimmie and Sally Pulliam, Seig and Dot Rush, Billy and Sassy Shull. The men had all been fraternity brothers at the University of South Carolina and were good friends. They all bought lots on the Circle and began building their homes in the next several years. Little did some of them think that these homes were going to not only be their homes but also their children were going to stay on the Circle and rear their families in these very same houses. The first family to build was the Pulliams in 1950, followed by the Dawsons and the

Rushes in 1955, and then the Shulls and Gaydens in 1957. The group founded The Bridge Club and started several traditions. One of the most fun traditions was on Christmas Day the children and their families would go visit all the different homes

to see what Santa had brought thus continuing to spread Christmas cheer. When one of these family members passed away, it was a loving tradition to have the Casket Spray made from greenery from their gardens on Spring Lake Circle.

Another group to build on the Circle were Walter and Betty Taylor, and Reginald and Isabel Heinitsh. Both had purchased lakefront lots on the Circle, with the Taylors having bought theirs in 1948. Walter and Isabel were cousins and the two families thought it would be very special for their children to grow up together. Both men built their homes on the lake in 1950. When Mr. Taylor brought his mother and mother-in-law to see the beautiful property on which he was planning to build his home, both women broke into tears. This was too far out in the country!

In 1954 Albert Heyward and his wife, Anna Belle, built their home next to the Taylors. 624 Spring Lake Road was built by Betty and Walter Taylor and has been continuously occupied by Taylors: first their daughter Elsie and her children, Blair and Eleanor and then their son, Walter and his wife, Helen, with their girls Sallie and Lizzie.

THIS PHOTO WAS TAKEN AT THE CELEBRATION FOR KAREN PULLIAM MANGE'S 60TH BIRTHDAY. ORIGINAL FAMILY MEMBERS AND CHILDREN OF ORIGINAL FAMILIES ATTENDED. THE ORIGINAL FAMILIES CONTINUE THE BOND.

<u>The Story of the Cherry Trees</u>

Spring Lake Circle residents from the earliest homeowners to the present have always enhanced Mother Nature by adding to the natural beauty of the long leaf pines, the inviting magnolias and the Carolina yellow jasmine. An interesting story occurred in the 1960's when Virginia Lentz had the idea of homeowners planting a flowering Yoshino Cherry tree in their yards, close to the road so that in spring the lovely blossoms could be seen and enjoyed by everyone living or visiting the Circle. Facts have it that she ordered the Yoshino Cherry trees from Taylor Garden Center and then sent a bill to the homeowners to pay for their trees. One male homeowner upon receiving the bill stated that he could purchase a good bourbon for that amount instead of a tree! Thanks to Virginia's love of blooming trees and planning some sixty-four years ago, these lovely cherry trees enhance the natural beauty of Spring Lake Circle and bloom each year for all to enjoy.

2

NEW TRADITIONS

Neighborhood Christmas Trees

In 1997, the Circle began the Neighborhood Christmas Tree tradition, which was organized by Jeannie Powell. This now has become a much anticipated and fun tradition with some neighbors racing to be the first one to have their tree up and decorated! Jeannie and her sister grew up in Florence, SC where the Neighborhood Christmas Trees had been a tradition as long as she could remember. Jeannie and her sister, Evie, wanted to start the beloved tradition in their own neighborhoods here in Columbia. Circle residents participate by putting up six-foot Christmas trees in their front yards. Decorated with large, opaque bulbs, the trees are a beautiful way to celebrate the holiday season. Christmas memories are made each year as families and friends ride around the Circle enjoying our colorful and festive trees decked out for the holidays.

Halloween Night Hot Dog Supper

The Halloween Night Hot Dog Supper was started in 1985. Circle Resident Laura Williams had enjoyed this Halloween fun event while she lived in Greenville, SC. She and Lillian Coleman organized the first Halloween gathering. Adults can come in costume or not, but children are always in costume for this spooky night of the year! Hot dogs are provided and everyone brings a side dish. After enjoying their supper, parents and their children head out to trick or treat the Circle residents. A popular stop was Colonel and Mrs. Richard Coulter's house where the Coulters would take a Polaroid picture of each Trick or Treater and then you were given a treat along with a picture to take home. It was a brave Trick or Treater who walked down the ghost inhabited driveway of the Joanne and Bill Campbell house and a scary witch was always behind the door at the home of Sandy and Michael Roberts, whose front yard is always filled with Halloween blowups for all to enjoy!

Annual Spring Lake Circle Picnic

The Annual Spring Lake Circle Picnic began in 1990. A group of folks living on the Circle thought it would be a good and fun idea to get together to celebrate the beginning of summer and  the completion, finally, of the yearlong pipeline installation on the Circle. The first two Family Picnics were held at the home of Linda and Bill Gillespie. Fried chicken was ordered and iced tea and lemonade were provided. Everyone brought a side dish to share. Guessing games and yard games were played by the children at the early picnics. Organizers for this event were Linda Gillespie, Jennifer Todd, Sharon Vanzant and Laura Williams. For years residents enjoyed their annual picnics overlooking the lake as several of the lakeside residents took turns hosting

the event. In 2021 the Picnic Organizers decided to do something different and serve BBQ instead of chicken. We are now able to enjoy delicious homemade BBQ provided by Circle Chefs Chuck Davis, Robert Belding and Bubba Ross. As in the past everyone brings a side dish to share. We get together outside between the homes of Libby and Sims Tompkins and Sharon and Pete Vanzant. This has been a fun time for all of us to enjoy catching up with the old neighbors and welcoming the new neighbors to the wonderful circle!

Ducks on the Lake -
Old and New Traditions

In the early years, 1950's and 1960's, Sammy Small (728) bought several dozen baby ducks every Easter. He and Jimmie Pulliam (716) built a duck coop in the Pulliam's yard by the lake. The children in the neighborhood, along with some adult help, fed and cared for the ducks until they could be released on the lake to survive on their own.

Taking care of wildlife on the Circle is still important and springtime can find Amanda Malanuk (640) rescuing small, baby ducks which have been abandoned near the lake. She rallies friends and neighbors together and delivers duck pellets for feeding until the ducks can care for themselves on the lake.

Amazon, Fed Ex, and UPS Thank You's

The Botstein Family has a tradition of helping others during the holidays by leaving a most inviting basket on their front porch. It offers the Amazon, FedEx and UPS delivery folks a choice of snack, water or other soda beverage as they speed along with deliveries from house to house through this neighborhood.

Winburn Annual Gatherings

Neighborhood Events hosted by Lara and Scott Winburn are Ice Cream Trucks, the Annual Easter Egg Hunt with the famous Easter Bunny available for pictures and the annual winter movie night. The children and adults enjoy these special events.

3

Memories from the Circle

I love our "New Traditions" like the trees in the yards at Christmas, the Halloween Party and the Spring Picnic. The Circle has always been a community. Created by a group of friends who wanted to raise their families together, including my parents, the Rushs, the Dawsons, the Shulls, the Gaydens, and the Pulliams. They were lifelong friends, who bought out in the "middle of nowhere" so they could be together. Now we are all doing the same for our families and I love it!

Back then, the Circle was really way out and when my father brought his mother to see where he was building his home for his family, she broke down in tears and asked, "Why do you want to live this far out in the country?" I am so glad he chose the Circle- I am the second generation to live in my house. The Circle will always be my home. It is the only place in Columbia to live!

The neighbors were really sweet to us crazy kids growing up on the Circle. The nicest lady, Miss Hancock (704) would always have those boxes of cubed sugar. We would ring her bell for a lump of sugar! Probably drove her crazy but you would have never known it!

The Kinnie family (619) had a pool and the Circle kids loved to swim in their pool. We would start calling Mrs. Kinnie first thing in the morning asking if we could come swim in her pool. She finally became tired of us calling her and bought a flagpole. When the flag was flying, it meant the pool was open for us kids and we could come down and swim!

When we Tricked or Treated, a very special stop was the house where Mrs. Isabel Whaley Sloan (628) lived. We were invited to wander the whole house looking for bowls filled with treats placed in the rooms. Of course, these hidden candies were the same ones Mrs. Sloan passed around during her dance lessons. All the kids took ballroom dancing from Mrs. Sloan. The Halloween candy was probably from the Candy dance!

The Davis family (740) had a real live monkey as a pet and the monkey would ride on the back of their German Shephard. We thought that was very exotic-like we were at the circus!

It was a great childhood on the Circle. We played in the creek, swam in it when it flooded from raining too much. Snuck onto the golf course when we had snow and sled down the hills; I am sure we messed up some of the greens, but we had fun! It was a wonderful childhood!

-Libby Rush Tompkins (727)

In the back yard of this house is a large structure affectionally known as the Green House by the present owners, Sharon and Pete Vanzant. This house was actually an Officers' Barracks Building at Fort Jackson, SC that was moved here in 1955 by the first owner of 731 Spring Lake Road, William

T. Dawson. It is a Small Barracks Building and could house four officers. While they were growing up here, the Vanzant children were convinced that the house was haunted, but there are no ghosts making their home in this house!

-Sharon Vanzant (731)

Spring Lake Road. These are powerful words to me, they mean home. "Take Trenholm. Take a right on Spring Lake. Follow the golf course, make every right turn and you will end up in my driveway." Home. The Circle. It is little over a mile, we in our family, fondly call "the loop." A place that after Thanksgiving a walk on the loop helps justify desserts. The right curves, no perfect curves and a place where a kid on a purple banana seat bike could roam. As a preteen there were no boundaries. Your yard was my yard. I loved to go to the Greenlee's pool, hidden and surrounded by trees. I never once thought about how they may look out the window and think, "What is Muffie Mitchell doing in our back yard?" Spending the night with Gigi Dawson, plays we put on for her mom and dad and Buttons, the dog. In the morning feasting on whatever we wanted for breakfast (Mrs. Dawson would cook for 5+ whatever we wanted.) Then on to Gigi's swing in the back yard to swing high on the swing set, singing to the wisteria that hung high in the pine trees.

The creek which was once beautiful. I played in the water, imagining different lands and green rivers and it was only in a sliver of a beautiful creek. It was a miracle that I wasn't bitten by a snake as I played in the water all day long. From one side of the loop at the lake, walking straight up the center of the creek. Free as an explorer on a hot summer day. When the rain was fierce and the creek would rise and spread across the Jennings side lot my brother would take a surf/kick board and ride the water under the pipe in the road. I was never brave enough...I left that to my brother, Bill and his friend, John Kinnie.

There were houses where you could stop by and ask for a candy (Mrs. Sloan at 628) or even a sugar lump (the sugar lump lady) There were doors I would knock on "just to chat" (Mr. Jennings, 550) and it was there I learned the difference between something's height and how high something was. Corrected in a discussion where I mixed up my verbiage I gave a note to self, "Mr. Jennings, lawyer, exact, vocabulary matters," got it!

My sister Kathy (child #3) tells the story that when I was born, she, as a 12-year-old, took me as a six-week-old baby down the street in her doll carriage to meet the neighbors. When they opened the door and saw the new baby they screeched "Does your mother know you have Muffie down here?"

"Yes! Mother said I could come!"

It got pretty loose by the time I (#8 child) came so I guess I come by the house to house traveling honestly.

As a teen I could drive Spring Lake Road in the pitch black dark and know where to turn with my eyes closed. Not wise but...I could probably still do it. I knew every tree and every bush. Where the scuppernongs grew on the fence to the golf course, who had my favorite cherry trees and who had the best magnolia to climb. There were 7 or 8 kids my age on the circle. What a gift to have friends all the way around that loop.

I am so thankful to have our family house back and to be able to restore it in a way I literally dreamed about for years. I feel my parents there as I walk the garden. Stripping back the house and the garden to its original beauty, I can imagine their excitement when they built it. I feel that same excitement as I rebuild it.

So, Spring Lake Circle if you see an old lady with flowers in her hair on a purple banana seat bike in your back yard, don't worry, it's only #8 of the Mitchell's!

-Muffie Mitchell Faith (604)

Growing up on the Circle was so much fun. In the beginning it was dirt, then gravel with tar (bumpy and you could not roller skate on it), finally asphalt. In those days, people did not cut down many trees. You could not see the house at 624 from the street. Most houses were also hidden among the trees on the lake side too. At night as we came in from skiing or boating, you could see all the lights peeking through the leaves. In the Spring, the Circle was a fairy land between the dogwood trees looking like snow and the cherry blossoms shimmering in the sun.

In summertime, every day was an adventure. We would get up in the morning and be gone all day until time for supper. Mrs. Heyward had a big black bell on a tall pole that she would ring at suppertime to call all the Heyward children home.

Anna Belle and I became close friends when she moved in next door at 616 when we were four years old. I often would invite her to spend the night. Because she was afraid to leave home, she would pack her suitcase and come for lunch. After lunch we had to nap so we put our pajamas on to practice. We would have a grand afternoon playing and having supper. However, once night came and we were in my bed, she could see the light on at her back door from my bedroom window and start crying. I don't think that she ever made a whole night until we were teenagers!

I was always at the Heyward's house. Often, I would join them at the dinner table (there were four children – Albert, Carroll, Anna Belle and Sarah). As Mrs. Heyward would serve plates, she would realize there was an extra child and she would say "Elsie, go home!"

The Shealy's lived on the other side of the Heyward's house. Mr. Shealy was a wonderful gardener, and his garden was full of secret rooms. Anna Belle and I loved to take our dolls over to play until Mrs. Shealy turned on the sprinklers to run us off.

When we were six, we both asked Santa for doll houses. Santa brought Anna Belle a tin two story doll house with plastic furniture. Elsie's arrived on a flatbed truck. It was white with a green front door and two windows which had white organdy curtains flocked with red hearts! It remained a beloved doll house until it became the home for two goats, named Anna Belle and Albert for the Heywards. Later it became a stable for our pony named Beauty. Unfortunately, Beauty was very mean and escaped every morning when we tried to feed her, so she did not last long! After that it became a clubhouse for us girls until the boys, Walter and Clement, took it over where they mostly smoked cigarettes.

There was a small pond behind the Jennings' house at 550 fed by a creek that runs from the golf course (where the club's maintenance sheds are) through the interior of the Circle (behind the Ellison's, Morgan's and Jennings' houses) and on into the lake. We were always playing in the pond and the creek. One summer Albert Heyward organized all the children to build a swimming hole behind John Morgan's house. We dug and dug and dug for days until Albert thought it was deep enough for a diving board. I don't remember anyone ever really diving but lots of people had to "walk the plank".

Around 10 or 12 years old, our mothers began to let us ride our bikes on Saturdays to the corner of Trenholm Road and Forest Drive. We rode across the golf course to Country Club Drive. From there we rode down John C. Cooper's driveway to come out on Old Mill and cross the bridge behind Forest Lake Shopping Center never having to go on a main road. We left our bicycles on the ground, got on the Fort Jackson bus and went to Main Street. There we ate either at Tapp's basement or the Quick Shop and then we went to a movie. When we returned on the bus, our bicycles were just where we had left them. We would buy jelly donuts at the bakery behind what is now Coplon's, play on the swings in the park and then ride on home!

-Elsie Taylor Logan (624) & Anna Belle Kibler (616)

No locks, no keys, no last names. They were always just Dee and Rudy, Sally and Jimmie, Dolly and Ames, Dot and Seig, Gretchen and Bill, Martha Ware and Sammy and Sassy and Billy. Our "sliver of the circle" and slice of heaven. We knew where the saltines were at the Gayden's, the homemade chocolate chip cookies were at the Wells' and the Root Beers and Charles Chips were at the Dawson's. We could walk in any time and help ourselves. (And we did.)

We moved onto Spring Lake Road in 1954 and our mother and Sandy, the youngest Shull girl, live there still. For our family, it was a bit like living in a commune. Our parents bought our lot when four of our father's closest friends bought theirs. Five families: the Dawsons, Rushes, Gaydens, Pulliams and Shulls were all in the same bridge club, had gone to the same high school, went to the beach together and had children all about the same age. So, we all knew that we didn't just have one set of parents who watched out for us, who would feed us, care for us and discipline us.

The bus stop was at the top of the Gayden's yard. There were probably 12 or 14 of us at that stop. Every year on the last day of school we could "take a friend" to school, on the bus, by ourselves. One year Sally took Libby Rush. She was about three years old; Sally was maybe seven! Libby made it back alive. Parents were a good deal more relaxed back then. There was always a kickball game after school in the Gayden's front yard. Boys and girls, old and young. There really was not a pecking order on the circle. We learned to ride a bike with no hands, with Evelyn Wells, and Leslie Gayden. We rode all the way around the circle, of course with a stop at Mrs. Hancock's for a cube of sugar.

At Christmas time, Sammy and Martha Ware Small housed Santa's workshop. They had older children and a huge walk-up attic that housed not only the best model train you can imagine but also everything that Santa planned to bring to all of us. Parents met Christmas Eve to get their loot. Once that was done, they all fixed a drink and toured the neighborhood to see each house while the children slept. Sammy also had a great dock and a boat. On the Fourth of July we caravanned boats down to Forest Lake Club to watch the fireworks.

Some of our most laughable memories involved our daddy, Billy Shull. The one we remember most vividly was all about tomatoes. Who could grow the biggest. Daddy and Sammy boasted they could grow bigger tomatoes than Rudy and Jimmy. Daddy knew someone who convinced him to drive to Sumter to pick up some special chicken poop- guaranteed to produce giant tomatoes. We rode with him, a big mistake. We did not own a pickup truck and will never forget the smell of that car! He and Sammy were so excited about this secret weapon until they walked out to burnt tomatoes. So...they snipped the bad tomatoes off the vine, found some beautiful tomatoes at the market and tied them on. We can still see them both crying from laughing so hard at out foxing Rudy and Jimmy.

So many laughs, so many memories. Growing up on the circle was idyllic and pretty simple. It has always been not just about family but about community. We felt safe but had lots of freedom ...and plenty of watchful loving eyes.   Lucky us!

-Sally Shull Teden, Hargrave Shull McElroy,
Sandy Shull Roberts and Sassy Shull (723)

4
Spring Lake Road Famous Residents

1. Leland "Lee" Allen Bandy | Journalist

Political journalist for South Carolina's *The State Newspaper*, Lee Bandy (418) spent 40 years covering not only South Carolina's political stage, but for two decades he was the chief Washington correspondent for the paper. Lee was known for his honesty, kindness, and ability to ask the right question, even if it was impertinent. Lee Bandy was a well-respected journalist in the political sphere who wrote 3,000 political columns, was a member of the Gridiron Club, and appeared frequently on national television.

2. Jimmy Buffet | Singer, Song-writer, & Musician

Circle resident Jane Slagsvol (636) met the *"Margaritaville"* singer, song-writer and musician in the 70s and they were married in 1977. They were married for over four decades and had three children together. Jimmy wrote his hit song, *"Come Monday"* for Jane while he was on the road and missing his then girlfriend, Jane Slagsvol.

3. Richard Mark Gergel | Judge of the US District Court

Richard Gergel (719) began his law career as a law clerk for a firm in Columbia, SC in 1979, becoming a partner in that firm from 1981 to 1982. Beginning in 1983 until 2009, Mr. Gergel was a personal injury lawyer, president, and partner at his own law firm. It was during this time period that he came to call the Circle his home. In December 2009, President Barack Obama nominated Mr. Gergel to serve on the United States District Court of South Carolina as a judge, which he was appointed to and still serves.

4. Mark Greiner and Grayson James Greiner | Basketball and Baseball Players

Mark Greiner (402) played basketball under legendary Coach Frank McGuire at the University of South Carolina from 1972-76 and his son Grayson played baseball for USC Baseball Coach Ray Tanner from 2012-2014. Grayson was drafted by the Detroit Tigers after his Junior year and made his big-league debut with the Tigers on May 6, 2018. He played close to five years in the big leagues.

5. Thomas Travis Medlock | 48th Attorney General of South Carolina, State Representative, & SC State Senator

Serving in the Democratic Party since 1965, Thomas Travis Medlock (703) was a public servant to the state of South Carolina for many decades. Mr. Medlock served in the South Carolina House of Representatives from 1965-1972, then moved to the State Senate from 1972-1976. 1983 saw Mr. Medlock serving as the 48th Attorney General for South Carolina and calling Spring Lake Rd his home. Though Mr. Medlock no longer calls the Circle his home, he is still fighting for the people in South Carolina as a personal injury lawyer.

6. Judge Roy Alexander Powell | Chief Municipal Judge

Judge Powell (628) served as Chief Municipal Judge of Columbia from 1974 to his retirement in 1980.

7. Ben Ross | Co-founder of Brackish

Ben Ross (619) comes from the Circle and in 2007 while preparing for his wedding had the idea to combine turkey feathers to his groomsmen's bowties for a unique thank you gift to his friends and family, as well as a unique wedding detail. In 2012 Jeff Plotner, one of the lucky groomsmen approached Ben to co-found a new business, Brackish and the rest is history. The Company is set in Charleston, SC and has expanded into women's accessories as well as holding true to the roots of men's bowties and other accessories.

8. Judge Alex Sanders | Chief Judge, South Carolina Court of Appeals, President of College of Charleston, Chair of the Board of Directors of the Charleston School of Law, Former SC State Representative and Former SC Senator

Judge Alexander Mullings Sanders, Jr. (406) served as a State House Representative from 1966-1974 and a State Senator from

1976-1983. Beginning in 1983 Judge Sanders was the Chief Judge of the South Carolina Court of Appeals until leaving the court to become the 19th President of the College of Charleston. In 2003 Judge Sanders and four other individuals started the Charleston School of Law, where he served as Chairman of the Board until 2013. Judge Sanders is currently practicing law with his daughter, Zoe C. Sanders, at the Sanders Law Firm of South Carolina.

9. June S. Shissias | SC State Representative

Former Social Worker, June S. Shissias (448), served in South Carolina House of Representatives from 1992-1996.

10. Isabel Whaley Sloan | Owner of Mrs. Sloan's Ballroom Dancing and Social Etiquette School

For over three quarters of a century several generations of Columbia's youth learn to dance and proper etiquette from Mrs. Isabel Sloan (628), including South Carolina's current governor, Henry McMaster. At just 17 years of age herself, Mrs. Sloan opened up her school in 1914. During World War II Mrs. Sloan organized dances and held social events for thousands of servicemen who were stationed at Fort Jackson.

11. Richard Louis "Dixie" Walker, Ph.D. | American scholar, Author, & Former Ambassador to South Korea

In 1957 Richard Louis "Dixie" Walker (700) moved to Columbia South Carolina to organize a new program in International Studies at the University of South Carolina. Dr. Walker founded USC's Walker Institute of International and Area Studies in 1961 and headed the program until 1981.

In 1981, 40th President of the United States of America, Ronald Reagan asked Dr. Walker to serve as ambassador to the Republic of Korea. Dr. Walker served with distinction until 1986, longer than any other American ambassador. He is credited with helping to secure the release of future South Korean president, Kim Dae-jung. President Reagan awarded Dr. Walker with the Department of Defense Distinguished Civilian Service Award.

After serving as ambassador Dr. Walker returned to USC and his first love of academia, writing and contributing to books that focused on cultural factors in international relations, especially in East Asia, until his death in 2003.

The Circle Homeowners Past & Present

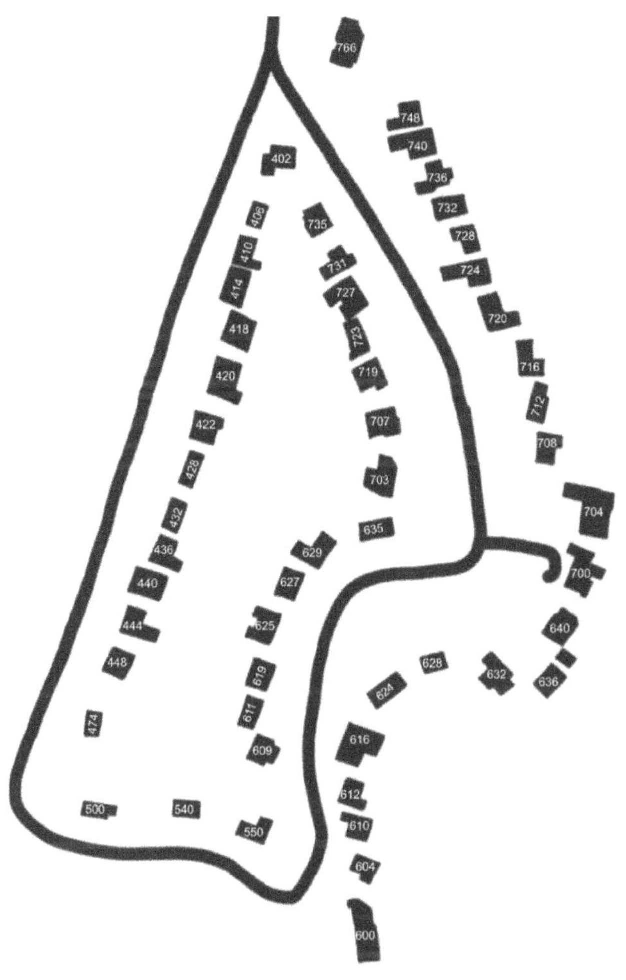

The following is a listing of the homeowners (current and past) on Spring Lake Circle.

Sassy Shull (723) currently lives in her home that she and Billy built in 1957. She is the only original homeowner still residing in her home.

Second generations living in the home where they grew up are;

Libby Rush Tompkins (727)   Zoe Sanders (406)
Jay Pulliam (716)   Hartley Powell (632)
Walter Taylor (624)   Dolly Coulter (732)

Bett Williams (422) Grandparents' home
Beau Powell grew up on the Circle and now resides (748)

There are a number of other homes that have had only two owners or owners who built on homesite which is quite remarkable for a period of 75 years.

Huntley (410)   Johnson (707)
Farrell (428)   Cribbs (712)
Todd (436)   Gillespie (720)
Shissias (448)   Vanzant (731)
Ellison (500)   Wise (736)
Simmons (610)   Morrison (766)
Ross (619)

Welcome to Spring Lake Circle!

First families to Spring Lake Road denoted with *

House Number	Year Bought	Owners
402	1955	Hartin, Rhett and Ruby Lee
		Oliver, Hampton and Ellen
	1986	Stuckey, Roy and Dale
	1995	Evans, Gregory
	1997	Greiner, Mark and Karen
	2002	Middleton, Richard and CeCe
	2014	Abuhashem, Omar
	2015	Winburn, Scott and Lara
406	1950	*
	1963	Sanders, Alexander and Zoe
	1998	Sanders, Zoe Caroline
410	1955	Thompson, Thomas
	1994	Huntley, Harry and Kathy
414	1969	Vaden, Charles and Jane
	1995	Turbeville, Bill and Mary
	2020	Cobb, Ryan and Charlotte

418	1950	*
	1983	Holler, William C
	1988	Clary, Chip and Lydia
	1992	Bandy, Lee and Mary
	2006	Parker, Patricia
	2009	Maas, Emmett and Andrea
420	1951	*Odom, Charles T
	1984	Loomis, Maxine/Wood, Delores
	1998	Moorman, John and Kirsten
	2001	Oliphant, Julia
	2005	Kopecky, Chris and Blake
	2016	Smith, Robert and Catherine McClung
422	1955	*Farrell, Wilson and Betty
	2001	Williams, Phillip and Bett
428	1954	*Hoefer, Mary Jewel and Carrington
	2016	Farrell, Charlie and Susan
432	1960	*deTreville, Paul and Marian
		Sullivan, Richard and Marian
	1984	Williams, David and Laura
	1995	Short, Bill and Sally
	2020	Crouch, George and Morgan
436	1967	Lot owned by Leon Goodall
	1992	Todd, Chuck and Jennifer

440	1967	Lot owned by Leon Goodall
	1997	Goodall, Chris and Linnell
	2014	Kopecky, Chris and Blake
	2016	Dover, Michael and Joanna
444	1963	*Lentz, John and Virginia
		Clare, Stuart and Henrietta
	1976	Tompkins, Linn S. Jr. and Linda
	1989	Burnett, Carey and Ann
	1991	Roberts, Michael and Sandy
448	1957	Brazell, Carl and Mary Alice
	1977	Shissias, George and June
474	1957	Wieland, Joanne and Bob
	1970	Hays, Hal and Linda
	1980	Brooks, Lovic A., III
	1986	Sandifer, Phil and Becky
500	1953	*Ellison, David and Cornelia
	1995	Ellison, Susan
540	1956	Hudak, Ronald
	1957	Morgan, John Jr.
	1982	Lovvorn, Dixon and Peggy
	1994	Peterson, Michael and Jan
	2007	Henderson, Jane Cobb

550	1950	*Jennings, W. Croft and Betty
	1978	Dawson, William T. and Gretchen
	2013	Brabham, Will and Margaret
600	1956	*Mitchell, Dr. Dana C. Jr. and Beaumont
	2001	Kennemur, Dennis and Mary
	2014	Strom, Pete and Susan
	2022	Faith, Muffie Mitchell
604	1958	*Mitchell, Florence Marie Beaumont
	1995	Williams, David and Laura
	2022	Faith, Muffie Mitchell
609	1983	Jennings, Ann R (lot)
	1993	Mann, Edward C. (Bud) and Genie
	2005	Davis, Chuck and Kathy
	2015	Oliphant, F. Murray and Mary Oliphant (Lockie)
	2019	Donley, Jonathan and Ashley Donley
610	1978	*Jennings, W. Croft and Betty
	1999	Simmons, Ken and Kathy
611	1955	
	1974	Richardson, Buddy and Janet
	1988	Matthews, Manton and Catherine
612	1954	*Shealy, H. A.
	1988	Powers, Winifred
	1989	Garris, Steve and Sally

616	1954	*Heyward, Albert and Anna Belle
		McCoy, Bob and Barbara
	1980	Ringley, Edward and Sara Ellen
619	1960	*Kinnie, Bruce and Jean
	1988	Ross, Fred (Bubba) and Julie
624	1950	*Taylor, Walter and Betty
	1983	Owens, Jimmy and Elsie Taylor
	2001	Taylor, Walter and Helen
625	1969	*Craig, Charles and Nita
	1976	Seibels, John and Judy
	1995	Laffitte, Tucker and Helen
627		Haynesworth, Liz
		Clark, Brandon
		Davis, Clarence and Rosalyn
	2010	Davis, Chuck and Kathy
628	1951	*Sloan, Isabel Whaley
	1987	Powell, Hartley and Jeannie
	1989	Cassels, Tobin and Pat
		Heinitsh, Reginald
	1995	Parsons, Monte
	2010	Davis, Clarence and Rosalyn
	2024	Foster, Mike and Laura

629	1955	*Meeks, Frank T. and Laura Mae
	1986	Coleman, John D. and Lillian
	1995	deLoach, John and Elizabeth
	2001	Matthews, Matt and Ann Marie
	2023	Greene, Rob and Catherine
632	1955	*Dreher, Clarence
	1962	Powell, Roy and Annabelle
	1989	Powell, Hartley and Jeannie
635	1956	Tolbert, Carl and Catherine
		Greenlee, Robert E., Jr.
	2002	Butler, Pierce
		Manning, Dibble and Carla
		Moore, David and Lindsey
	2019	Botstein, Jonathan and Kendra
636	1950	*Heinitsh, Reginald and Isabel
	1968	Slagsvol, Thomas and Sally
	2007	Mann, Bud and Genie
	2015	Walker, Joe and Haley
640	1951	*Malone, Guy
		Dixson, Francis Rogers and Norma
	1985	Campbell, and Bill and Joanne
	2004	Malanuk, Rob and Amanda

700	1952	*Nash, John and Susanna
		Walker, Ambassador Richard and Ceny
	2003	Smith, Bill and Beth
	2019	Tompkins, Jason and Kristin
703	1951	*Dixson, Francis Rodgers and Norma
	1984	Medlock, Travis and Laura
	1996	Davis, Chuck and Kathy
	2003	Borden, Michael and Julie
	2022	Bonyata, Nick and Heyward
704	1950	*Hancock, William and Claire
	1984	Hancock, Martha
	1991	Hancock, Bill
	2013	Goodall, Chris and Linnell
707	1959	*Wells, Ames and Dolly
	1993	Johnson, Marc and Sally
708	1950	*Hancock, Martha (lot)
	1988	Whaley, Roger and Allison Gayden
	1997	Crawford, Fred and Melanie
712	1950	*Herbert, Heloise and Beverly
	1986	Cribbs, Ashton and Mary Ruth
716	1950	*Pulliam, Jimmie and Sally
	2000	Pulliam, Jay and Susan

719	1950	*
	1951	Alexander, Grace H. and Bob
	1984	Gergel, Richard Mark and Belinda
	1990	Wilson, Dr. William D., Jr.
	2014	Crosthwaite, Suzanne Morris
	2018	Cooler, Arthur W.
720	1957	*Gayden, Rudy and Dee
	1984	Gillespie, Bill and Linda
723	1957	*Shull, William Dewey and Sassy
724	1952	*Carter, Red and Mary
		MacDonald, Mack and DeeDee
	1984	Adams, Milton
	1995	Hancock, Robert M and Elizabeth M.
	1996	Jernigan, John and Bobbie
	2004	McLean, Jodie and Pierre deLucy
	2019	deHoll, Doug and Susan
727	1955	*Rush, Seig and Dot
		Tompkins, Sims and Libby Rush
728	1951	*Small, Sammy and Martha Ware
	1970	Benton, Jimmie B.
	1990	Belding, Robert and Anne
731	1955	*Dawson, William and Gretchen
	1978	Vanzant, Pete and Sharon

732	1973	*Coulter, Richard and Margaret
	1998	Coulter, Dolly
735	1953	*Hayden, Bunny and Lynn
		Hemphill, Frank D. and Marvis
		Narr, Yves and Martine
	1993	Brown, Paul and Beverly
	2001	Stafford, Bob and Sarah
	2020	Rush, Tripp and Sara Beth
736	1955	*Walker, Robert, Sr.
		Walker, Cosmo
	2020	Wise, Andy and Stacy
740	1953	*Davis, Wilton H.
	1993	Deierlein, Jim and Jane
	2016	Bunch, Lucas and Kelly
	2018	Bunch, Robert and Gail
748	1958	Miller, Ben N. (lot)
	2016	Powell, Beau and Alice
766	1958	*Miller, Dr. Ben N. and Ruth
	1992	Morrison, Sid and Meg

Photo credits:

- First Families left side, second paragraph: Bill Dawson and Jimmie Pulliam
- First Families right side, second paragraph: The Rush Family
- First Families right side, third paragraph: Betty Taylor and Isabel Heinitsh
- First Families left side, third paragraph: Walter and Betty Taylor
- First Families final photo: (first row, left to right) Sassy Shull, Sally Pulliam, Dolly Wells, Gretchen Dawson (second row, left to right) Hargrave Shull McElroy, Allison Gayden Whaley, Jay Pulliam, Karen Pulliam Menge, Katon Dawson, Sandy Shull Roberts, Elsie Taylor Logan
- Halloween Night Hot Dog Supper: Halloween 2022
- Annual Spring Lake Circle Picnic: 2023
- Winburn Annual Gatherings: Easter Egg Hunt April 3, 2021
- Memories from Around the Circle left photo: Original backyard structure at 731
- Memories from Around the Circle right photo: Painted backyard structure at 731